The Dark Bark
Poetry and Song of Rin Tin Tin

CONTAINING A VARIETY OF INFORMATION RESPECTING THE ARTS AND
THE HISTORY OF THE TWENTIETH CENTURY.

Edited by Joe Green

Published by Owl Oak Press

101 Calle de Quien Sabe, Carmel Valley, CA 93924

USA©

ISBN: 0-9770380-3-3
Second Printing: 2017

DEDICATION

For Rusty... forever.

Remember the white buffalo!

CONTENTS

ACKNOWLEDGMENTS

Some of the poems chosen here first appeared in Fulcrum 2004 and Perihelion and are in whole or part so represented with permission of the editors at large.

Special thanks to Sufi Master Tim Smith for channeling Orson Welles.

INTRODUCTION TO THE RIN TIN TIN POEMS

These few poems are from the original 1,673 page manuscript "The Dark Bark" found buried in "The Yard" (as the poor animals who are to be euthanized call it) at the pound in Brighton Beach. They are the work of Rin Tin Tin. I write elsewhere of the strange and tragic events that led me to this manuscript – my depression, initial contacts with the spirit world, inadvertent destruction of the complete posthumous poems of Shakespeare as communicated to me by the spirit Elizabeth Barrett Browning, the establishment of communication with the dead animal world (Thank you, Ted Hughes) and, finally communication with Rinty's spirit with the assistance of the KA of W.H Auden.

Here I can only give the briefest sketch of Rinty's life.

We know about Rinty and the movies. I'll skip that. What is not so well known is that he was an excellent jazz guitarist. He met Billie Holiday in the Fifties. They fell in love. No one knew.

 Intellectual love, of course.

He goes mad with grief after her death and -- because all dogs know the essential existentialist insight -- decides to create himself anew by joining the Cuban revolution.

It doesn't work -- he tries to establish serious theatre in Cuba and overcome the typecasting he has suffered from all of his life.

Oh, during the first flush of revolutionary joy audiences accept him (he thinks) as Puck in his Marxist version of "A Midsummer Night's Dream" but soon he is reduced to playing bit parts in proletarian dramas and then its not long before there is no place for him in the State Theatre.

He works as a street performer for a bit -- usually as Lenin -- for the Soviet visitors Castro welcomes to the island. But then is arrested for anti-revolutionary activity when he tires of doing Lenin and tries a stint as Trotsky. After his release he makes his living --such as it is -- teaching the mambo to canine candidates for the Cuban National Circus and peddling marijuana to vacationers from Bulgaria.

In 66 he makes his move and escapes to NYC disguised as Chiquita Banana (he never says what happened to the young girl on the cruise ship who had been playing the part) and almost at once falls in with a crowd of drunken stand-up comic wannabes and, while stoned and driving a dune buggy along the beach, runs down and kills poet Frank O'Hara.

(O'Hara died of injuries he received when he was hit by a vehicle on the beach at Fire Island, on Long Island, New York).

He flees to Cuba.

He is caught and sentenced to prison again where he is released by Castro -- one of the hardened criminals Castro sends to the US -- where, after many adventures, he attains his dream and is acclaimed as the "Hamlet of his Generation" by NY theatre critics.

He gives it all up again and travels in Texas and

Mexico playing country guitar and getting in fights arguing over whether Fredric Remington or De Kooning is the best artist.

Gives that up and moves back to NYC. His poetry begins to be known.

The reader will note that in one sequence of poems Rinty claims to have assassinated JFK. True – he did testify before the Warren Commission but I believe we can dismiss these claims as sheer fantasy caused by Rinty's failure to get the lead role in "The Manchurian Candidate." I believe we should choose to remember the famous "Life" cover of Rinty saluting the eternal flame at JFK's tomb rather than those photos taken later that night on the Mall -- drunken, under arrest and wearing only a significant leer and a leopard-skin pillbox hat.

Rinty spent his last years in New York City.

And then, of course, destroyed by his own loathing of his being in time as a dog all he has left -- loveless and writing this memoir in the pound in Brighton Beach where he will be euthanized -- are memories of his betrayals and regrets that overwhelm everything else.

The first poem "Late for a Poetry Reading" starts
somewhat towards the end.

THE POEMS

Late for a Poetry Reading

Late for a poetry reading
and trusting the Sufi
livery cab driver
because he pretended
he knew me
(How old are you
anyway? What is that
in dog years?)
and half drunk
in any case
having known
intellectual love
with Billy
She dead these
thirty years
and fame and
an excess of revolutionary
ardor those years
in Cuba
and don't even
ask me about the sixties
having ridden the
Union Pacific
to the Cheyenne cutoff
loveless
in America
in winter

dreaming a
heavenly chasm
but no and
then hating
death and all
those who love it
returning through
West Texas from
Pancake to
Goodnight
in the railroad yard
there I heard
the OJays and
so returning to New York
and ending that night
somewhere in
I think
Long Island
poetry reading
in the Bronx
and at dusk
trying to find
my way back
seeing at the
window of
a perfectly bourgeois
house her a
young German Shepherd
the cream gold
glittering of her
eyes she looking
at this old dog
in perfect indifference
and knowing never
again I turn

the corner
always forever
going no-where
at the end of this
life

and bark
at the difficult dark.

Los Marielitos

You know Elmore Leonard
got a lot of his Florida schtick from me
when I was sobering up down in Miami.

I guess it was inevitable that I would
get involved with the mob after I fled Cuba
but it didn't start out that way.

May, 1980. They called us Los Marielitos.

I was one of 123,000 new Cuban refugees
that came to the USA in a short five months,
including about 5,000 of us who
were said to be hard-core criminals.

They crossed the ocean on a prayer.

On crowded, unsafe fishing boats.
On rafts held together by tires.

In search of a myth. Carrying only the
clothes on their backs, a passport, and a
crumbled piece of paper with a relative's phone number in the US.

I knew better.
The myth was over for me long ago.

I had Lassie's phone number but of course I would never call it.
She was probably dead and it was a whole new generation and
here I was, the icon of a previous generation, puking half-digested red
beans over the side of a raft.

Back in the USA. Back in the USA
done in by the hype back then and by,
yes, my own yen to do serious theatre.

"The Defiant Ones"

The studio really wasn't happy with Tony Curtis
His real name?
Bernie Schwartz.

They came to me. As always.

But I didn't really think it would be a good move
to play a role in which I would have
to be manacled to another actor for the whole movie.

I didn't tell this to Billy.
But she would have understood.
We had that kind of relationship.

"Don't threaten me with love, baby.
Let's just go walking in the rain."

I was already leery of typecasting
and ready to break out.

This was in 58, of course.
Billy died next year.
I remember what she told me:

"You can be up to your boobies in white satin,
with gardenias in your hair and no sugar cane
for miles, but you can still be working on a plantation."

Yeah, so my TV show was a hit.

5

So what?

West Side Story had been a possibility
It's based on Romeo and Juliet
but I turned that down too.

They didn't know about me and Billy.
Lady Day.

No-one did.

If they only knew.

Sidney Poitier was a gentleman to me when
I met him but I felt that... well...
that he simply wasn't up to the role

and I was tired of having to carry my part
and everyone else's'.

I suggested Richard Burton -- a little make up
... but they wouldn't go for it.

Sir Lawrence Olivier would have been good
But tell you the truth I didn't want to be chained to a lisping Limey for
hours on end.

And I'll tell you what.

It was Shakespeare or nothing.
That's the way I felt.

I told Billy I loved her.

She said:.

"Don't threaten me with love, baby.
Let's just go walking in the rain."

No, I Am Not Prince Hamlet Nor Was Meant To Be

You humans are so predictable.

In fact for years most dogs
were convinced that you were utterly
without self-consciousness -- without Mind.

After all, we present a stimulus to you
and we ALWAYS get a predictable response.

The fact is we have such a horror

of the fact

that we can NOT be sincere
that we do whatever we can
to make it stop.

Yeah, a dog will pant
and bark and bring the
damn ball back again and again and again

-- we do it to keep from going mad,
to hope to experience
just for an instant unmediated

unironic consciousness, to --for just one instant
-- be THERE, be in the moment.

It never works.

Never.

That's why we die so young
and it is also why I was,
on a foggy evening OFF OFF Broadway
in a little theatre in the year 1959,

I was, simply put,

the best Hamlet of my generation.

1953

1953 was a hard year for me.
Sad. I don't know why.
I had work. Me and Bob Mitchum
Were friends at last. After all
Those misunderstandings. "You want to
Break out?" I asked him. "Then forget
All this crap about being a natural actor."
I took his drink away. Got his attention.
"Acting is a craft. Don't scowl at me.
You know I'm right. You'll never
Do Shakespeare unless…" He eyed me warily.
"Yo, Rinty," he said. "You have Billy"
(I had told him) "What do I have?"
He fired up another Chesterfield.
Squinted through the smoke.
"Nothing happens anyway."

Nothing happens?
I knew what he meant.
I was getting there.

He grinned. "How the Hell did you
Do that to McCarthy?"
I gave him back his drink.
"Told him I was a commie, that's how.
"I'm an American Icon, Bob. It was too much for him.
Goodbye Tailgunner Joe."

Bob laughed but he didn't believe me.

He was really quite a charming man
Guys who don't believe in anything often are.
So he could be a gentleman to Rita Hayworth
Down in Mexico, her mind gone. But...
A bastard to everyone else.
Nothing in his eyes.

And I was sad there.
It was New York. September 13, 1953.
Another dive, Another gig.
Bob left with a blonde before I began to play.
I started to play but just walked out.
It was the night Jimmy and Tommy Dorsey had
Finally gotten together again.
They kept playing while I put down my guitar.

They never forgave me.

"A" train to Harlem.
Got in Billy's DeSota and drove.

In a few hours
Lost in Pennsylvania.
Stopped. Don't know why.
Got out. Looked up. Falling star.
Not me. Something from forever.

Finally found a town.
Asked a little guy outside a hospital for directions.
"We just had a baby girl," he said.

I drove back to my life.

In Loneliest Country

In Loneliest Country
I remember that
The philosopher Berdyayev wrote
About how when he
Was little and it was night
And he was with his mother
Wanting to get to Moscow
In a bolshoy hurry whizzing under
The stars in a sleigh the kind
Dear to the memory of Nabokov
That is a sort of unreal sleigh
As he was whizzing past all
Those wretched villages maybe
Seeing only a dog shivering
Before some wretched hut that
He thought All over
All over No More All lost
He would never see that dog again.

But I was worried there
In Loneliest Country
Warrensville, Pa turning
The corner of Second Avenue
Noticing a three legged dog
Following me and seeing it all
Someone's dead grandmother
Passed me and I was looking
For the Loneliest Ranger wondering who is
That lonely and restless man

Behind that swinging facade?
The dog following me the American Icon
And no Mister though
You never asked you smoking
A Pall Mall in front of the
Furniture store across from
Lipkins I don't need a 21 Inch
Magnavox Color TV or a bedroom soot.
And where was Loneliest I'll bet
In Cuernavaca or Taxco
Up the street I am wearing my
Sheep shirt the one with all
The sheep on it. Damn dog.
Turning up the Knowledge of Death
Is the Source of our Praise Avenue.

Unreal city and there he is
But I don't even have to ask
He says Behind that swinging facade
Is another swinging facade and
Then Do you remember the little cake
Shop on the Neva the one Pound mentions
Where he never was where I never was
Where you never was and I say
Damn right I do mofo
And he is gone and I turn to
The little three legged dog
Running TOWARDS me and
I am happy and call
"Here, Hoppy! Come here, boy!"

L.A. Song

It's all pre-need as they say.
I knew it when I went to L.A.
To lend my peculiar grace
To that particular place.
I'm sorry that I had to stay.

It's the wanting it all that kills.
Still, I wish I had one of them stills
Of me "In the Yukon"
With that little toucan.
I'll never see it and no-one else will.

I had a few drinks with my pals.
We wished we knew more of those gals.
Those gals who are sad
And wasted and bad.
The gals who were just like my pals.

So I stay in the Hollywood Hills.
And dream of the ghosts of those pills.
The kind you would take
At the Sir Francis Drake
And wait while the emptiness fills.

Breakfast at Tiffany's

And Capote there. Drunk in the morning.
That light is really what I remember
Through the window the jewels there.
Who was he anyway? Killings in Kansas.
"This is big, Rinty. I'm going to write about it.
Something new. Show them all."
Looking around tee he
To see who else was there.
Me looking at that light
"Look. Are you going to interview me or not?"
"A whole family. They killed them all.
Look I have a picture."
"I'm not looking at that," I said
And I was gone.

****

We were talking about Indians.
At the highway rest stop
You saw a stellar jay
Flying into the dark.

All these towns built on the bones
Of sleepy children!
Families hauling European clocks
Over the hourless prairie.

Into the dark again and the moon.
We stop even though it is below zero.
Something blows through our bodies.
Ghosts fleeing us. They can do this easily.

Tonight we finally see our bodies.
The moon's moon floats in the sky.
All night this happens!

****

What do you hear on the radio radio?
What do you hear on the radio, dear?

****

It was Christmas on Fifth Avenue
Ghost dog. Ghost dog.
I do this a lot.
I would save them all if I could.

Then I remember I left Capote with the check.

And I am happy again!

The green so green tree at Rockefeller Center.
Some guy telling a joke.
And I'm still hungry.
A Reuben and an egg cream.
The little waiter looking like God
His wife dead
Everyone a stranger forever.

The Thing

The Thing that
Is really
Quite unrepresentable
I represent anyway
It's really
Quite tenable
Just like a lawyer
Whose client
Unkennable
Testified awfully
Horribly unmendable
Admitting something
Really unpennable
An unkennable, unfencible
Horrible thing.
Really quite venerable
Completely unlexible
Sadly unhexible.

You say that I represent nothing at all?
Please, make yourself comfortable.
I'll go make a call.

RinTinTology

I never met Django
Never really wanted too, I guess
We would have "eyed each other warily"
Like the time I met Senator Jack Kennedy
Was it 57?
In the Cozy Cole me playing there
Jack with Sammy
Sammy told me he was nervous.
Jack working on his charisma thing
And me.. height of my fame
Billy there Jack wanting her to come to his table
Her not noticing and me looking at her
Playing "Vous et Moi"
Sammy said "Man, come on down see who's here."
So afterwards I sit down next to the Senator
He in black glasses smoking a Kool
Undercover or something
Billie came over. She said she liked the man
Afterwards, knew his Daddy... called him
Mr. Death. "That boy has troubles"
She said. "He was just nervous meeting me"
I told her. She could see that.
Anybody could. "He eyed you warily
Behind those shades" We laughed.
Forgot about it. I had something he wanted.
And he had something...something...
Held back... connection to.. as if he knew
About us, about me and Billy,
Something he said. Joking about Howard Hughes.

Sammy told me Jack laughed afterwards.
"Said he was nervous. Something strange. Didn't
Know why."

In 63 in August Castro "eyed me warily."
A little moonlight, bourbon on his breath,
Backstage, the little moon a paper one
For "Midsummers Night Dream" A wood near
Athens and I had transformed it, a bit of Brecht,
All of Shakespeare, Theseus nervous knowing
That Quince knew, Flute knew, Bottom breaking
the frame, declaring the revolution and me as Puck
Leaping, flying off that stage, like Peter Pan
TO FIDEL he standing up, smiling,
Me kneeling with the flowers but he
Afterwards backstage distant and cold wondering I thought
If the applause was for him or me.

Che was very nice, however.
Speaking one word... one word.
And I was in Dallas next was in Dallas then.

If I could play great jazz guitar
No hand...only paws.
Why couldn't I
Slowly, hold breath, there he is
Pull the trigger
Of a Manlicher-Carcano 6.5mm rifle?

The Platinum Goddess

Stepping into
Her room
I see
What should
Not be seen.

Beauty is sleeping.
Beauty is sleeping.

Nice work, my friends.

In Texas

Driving through
West Texas there
Ahead a silver trailer.
"Good Sam Club."
A dolt with a halo.

Passing on
The shoulder going
Nowhere I look up.
American dolt behind
the wheel.

Going nowhere.
Like me.
I can do nothing for him.

Arlington

Me standing before
The eternal flame.
Photogs.
Speed graphic cameras.
One tear.
Saluting Jack.
"American Icon"
Cover of Life

Yes, one wants life.
Nou goeth sonne under wod.

What a Little Moonlight Can Do

Three days after Bastille day
Behind the shut up café
In a broke down car
(Hard to gas yourself
If the car won't start)
In Cross Plains, Texas
Thinking I saw nothing
More than myself
Reflected in my Les Paul
Black Beauty that night
I step out of my 1971
Ford Maverick the
Door operated courtesy
Light snicking on and
Look up at the sky
At all the tired animals
Stars bluewhitelonely
Thinking of that night
At the Three Deuces so
Long Ago and playing at
The Famous Door
The night Billy died
Errol Garner, Me, Oscar
Pettiford, Errol saying
You better than Django
But nobody will ever say it.
Not knowing Billy was dead
I was happy. Looking up
I say at the skyey animals

The old dog in the moon
Ending like this
Saying to the drunks
In the cowboy bar
This riff is based on Les Negres
By Jean Genet laughing
At myself really and now
Wanting it to end but
The car won't start. Looking
Up I remember I told Billy
Radiance is the dealbreaker
And heard, radio definably off
Her singing "What a Little
Moonlight Can Do" and
That was the last time
I was truly happy and
I was there knowing
I would never try
To find the music again

Tired.

Pancake

Levelland

Mule Shoe

Sonora

Meadow

What vistas of hidden forgetfulness
Exhaustively at hand!

After the First Death, Well….

The collies yapped outside the funeral home
The whole world it seemed was sinking, sinking
I illumed the lamp, read a curious tome
Minnie Cheevied it and kept on drinking.
Damned hard to do with the goblins chuckling.
Ah, yes they won't get no satisfaction.
No swoons, or faints, and no knees buckling:
I read, and drink and choose inaction.
"More Ovaltine?" Lassie draws near.
"And tell me, Rinty, what are you reading?"
"It's only Captain Midnight, dear
Poor guy, he's taking quite a beating."
I kissed her, then said, "I won't forget
Though really screwed, he's not dead yet.

All the Starry Animals

Looking up
I love them too --
All the starry animals.
Looking down
Or not.
Not saying anything.
Not saying nothing either.

23

Road Kill

I ignore them.
The possum squashed on the macadam.
The unprophetic groundhog, in Texas
A holocaust of Armadillos, the skunk
"Skunk. God!" you say.
Driving on, a snake absolutely flat on the road.

There is no heaven of animals
A rabbit. A black and white cat.
A small dog stinking in the sun.

You see them and you make up a story.
The dog setting out to warn us all:
Fire, fire in the forest! The turtle there
100 years old!... what thoughts there, Rinty?
And what innocence for all of them.

I'm glad one of us knows the signs
To find our home.

Boulez, Bloch, Maurice Ravel

Boulez, Bloch, Maurice Ravel
Tell me. Are you doing well?
I seem to hear a faint demurral.
Is that you?
Or just this squirrel
Shivering in my winter garden
While I stand here like Sydney Carlton?

Mercy for all in fall of sparrow?
Do I hear a faint Bolero?

Letter from a Dog Before Troy

Dear Penelope,

It's windy here. Nine years in a tent on the beach.
Ulysses says they know what they're doing.

Right.

Nine years and for what?
What's nine years to them?

Most of my life.
I'm tired. Don't even ask me about the gods.
There's a limit to loyalty.

But you already know that.

I know about the puppies.
You should have told me.
She told me, of course.
I don't care.
Just get them out of Ithaca.

By the time you read this
I'll be gone. I have..what..four more years?
Going to someplace where there are no men.
No gods.
Maybe a few rabbits.

Old Dog: A Villanelle

I am an old dog and am gently trying,
To meekly go to the difficult dark..
Alone, alone I am slowly dying.

The slow snow drifts down and no wind sighing.
Take out a Zippo and light up a Lark.
No regrets none. No who and no whying.

Sad ghosts outside I hear them all crying.
Mort Sahl's on TV. Makes a funny remark.
No, thanks Time/Life I guess I'm not buying.

Death's at the door. The bastard is lying.
"Hey, Rinty! It's Lassie!" One small sad bark.
Wilder wind now. The snowflakes are flying.

Good Night has come. There is no denying.
Unknown is that country. Stark is the bark.
I am an old dog and am dying, dying.

And you, who haunt me forever sighing,
Crying my name in the difficult dark.
I am an old dog and am dying, dying.
I am alone and am dying, dying.

I am an old dog and am dying, dying.
I am an old dog and am dying, dying

Alone, alone I am slowly dying
I am alone and am dying, dying.

New York City--Towards Night

When I reflect how that
My little light went out
Ere I had a chance to
Be Poet Laureate
Then I find my mind returning ever
To the Golden Retrievers
Of Manhattan
Forced into the indignity
Of limping beside
The jogging wife
Of the Day Trader
With her highlighted tresses
And DKNY shirt
And her pierced low carb belly
Exposed and that bitter breed
Chained next to her
Desiring only, perhaps,
To die
Then only then
Am I at peace with Death.

I Died In New York

I died in New York
At the shelter in Brighton beach.
My last silence.
I thought of Pound at Rapallo in the last years.
Silence. He didn't speak to anyone.
He too had been in a cage.
Like him I wrote and wrote
It was all I had left.
1,673 pages of my life.
And this is how it ends.
The guy gave me part of his pastrami sandwich.
I had Lou Reed's number.
I had Woody's.
But I didn't ask the guy to call.

"Come, kindly death," I wrote.
Not without irony...it's a line I never got to say.
The kind of line that went to others.

I acted with my body one arf one twitch of the tail
and you knew what it meant to be with the 7th at Little Big Horn your
little boy dead beside you with a hole in his neck and the bright blood
and the blue sky above and

the

red

Indian

yowling and you running to tell someone, tell Custer
tear his throat out for he brought you to this

and then they'd say "CUT" and I would have a smoke and mess around
with my stand-in and tell Jew jokes and then

I

WAS

ON

but I never even began to be what I was

Never

Never

Never

and yes I could have been Lear.

Oh you are men of stone!

But I said not a word.

It's cold with the breeze from the beach.
I was in Brighton Beach
I was dying.

At Sardi's in 57 I think with Capote I told him
everything Hollygolightly and he took it and
changed the name to Tiffanys just because no-one
would believe a dog could be so tender and gay...

But I loved the movie.

It was cold in Brighton Beach
The guy also gave me some knishes.
All of it lost. I should have been kinder.

At night I howled.

My Epitaph

How oft has the Banshee cried
O'er a poor dead dog's grave?
Snow. Silence. Don't ask why.
Nothing to save.
Yet, I loved you sweet passers by.
Dear Catchers in the Rye.
As you are so once was I.

Jazz Life/Afterlife

I went to Hell.
Never looked back.
Already been to Texas.

Talk about "Le Jazz Hot."
They were all there.
Of course.
The Hot Club.

Like before...they were ghosts.

I remember that time in the Four Aces
Erroll saying. "You on tonight, my man"
Without irony.
I knew what he meant.
Laying down a line like Judassilver.
Wanting it all never getting it.
Missing that one chord.

He meant I wasn't perfect.
So perfect. So trying..like we all did.
Him what...in a few years?
Dead.
Love in vain.
All in vain.
And not

There... not getting it all
Just missing.

Notes dying.
Only rain outside.

Talk about "Le Jazz Hot."
They were all there.
Of course.
The Hot Club.

Before Another Poetry Reading

1.

Just like Robert Lowell
Before he went definably mad
My "author" (let's call him Joe) steps off the plane
Where he is met
With greasy servility
By a nervous graduate student
Who notes
Shaky hands
Red eyes
Too many whiskeys.
Into the car
"Reception at five, sir!"
"Five o'clock in the afternoon?"
Where are the great finned cars of yore?
Passels of Passats....only...
Joe eyes him warily.
"Take me to the Old Aquarium!"
"But...where?"
"I need to see the Colonel."
Vonnegut on the car radio. Still alive then?
"South Boston. I wait

For the blessèd break."
"Where...?"
"Drive," he says and somehow

There.

2.

"I have been living at the Garden of Allah.
Yours, Scott Fitzgerald"

Then
in the Wordsworth Room
Of the Pierce Brothers mortuary
1941 720 West Washington Boulevard
Ghost Dog
Returning to where I never was
Where was I?
Scott there. No.
"His hands were horribly wrinkled and thin."
At 44: "He actually had suffered and died an old man."
Returning then. Dorothy Parker remembers Gatsby
Says "Poor son of a bitch." to Scott Not Scott.
No there there as they say.
Seeing what? Mystery. Seeing what she wanted.

Ghost Dog.

"Scott, I will always remember looking in on
whatever it is that is to me, you.

Yours, Rin Tin Tin"

3.

At the monument.
Remembering that line about Shaw's father.
Looking for Loneliest there, perhaps.
Joe then back in the car.
"I'm ready," he says.
Shaky hands, red eyes..
"It's almost five. I don't know if we'll make it."
"Skunk hour," Joe thinks.
"Drive like the wind," he says.
Relinquunt Omnia Servare Rem Publicam.

Epigraph

I bark at at the dark until the darkness yields.
As you go stark. Babbling of green fields.

Yours,

Rinty

THE INTERVIEW WITH ORSON WELLES

ANNOUNCER

Ladies and gentlemen, the director of the Mercury Theatre and star of these broadcasts, Orson Welles.

ORSON WELLES: Hello, the Jeunesse Doree and all the ships at sea and in the maelstromed starry welkin!

This is ORSON WELLES.

Our interview tonight is with Rin Tin Tin The Great --. renowned actor (said to be the greatest Hamlet of his generation), author of **The Dark Bark**, Djangoiste and raccoonteur extraordinaire. On this particular evening the Crosley service estimates that thirty-seven point 239 billion creatures, mortal and immortal, are listening to us on their Zenith Trans-Cosmic radios. Zut alors!

ORSON: Mr. Tin Tin, or should I use Rin Tin Tin, or Rinty or...?

RTT: Call me anything. Just don't call me late for dinner. Ah, Orson...Rinty...just call me Rinty.

ORSON: We share a great many things in common Rinty; we are men of the world, masters of our various crafts, romantics at heart, and, above all else, lovers of the fine beautiful. You once loved Lady Day, Billie Holiday, I once loved Judy Holiday. Despite your TV work, you were essentially a noiriste. The synchronicity of it! Will you tell us how you came to who you were? Lets begin with your dam and sire, shall we?

RTT: I never knew them, Orson. I'm an orphan and I am an American, Chicago born. I guess my real name is Moishe Herzog, Junior. Yeah, I'm a dog but I never even saw a dog until I saw Hettie in Buffalo Bill's Wild West Show when it came to town. I was already seven years old! In fact I thought "dog" was my name. My owner was Moishe Herzog and I grew up in the back of his pawnshop. "Here, dog," he would say whenever he wanted to show me something in the Torah or more often to go down into the basement and get him a book or to bring up one of the lariats he would use to practice his rope tricks.. He was a strange guy. And, of course, so was I. All I knew was the pawnshop, the Torah, the Hebrew Spinoza and a variety of rope tricks. Though Moise would kill me for not saying "lariat." He was a great fan of the Wild West.

Here's how it all started.

Picture this my friend. It's round midnight in Chicago and snowing -- I could see the flakes softly falling through the pawnshop window, no cars then so it's quiet, a hush. I am trying to sleep and not to sleep -- every night I had to go into the basement and bring up an old horse blanket and spread it right beneath the window. "Watch the shop, dog," Moishe would say as he left -- so this is how I thought I was to do it. Every night I tried to stay awake to watch the shop. Of course, I couldn't so when Moishe would come in the next morning and ask "Did you watch the shop last night, dog?" and I gave a little yap indicating, I guess, that I had, I felt incredibly guilty. He never seemed to notice that I was lying but I still felt guilty as hell.

Well, that night I was determined to stay awake and tried everything.

I was determined to memorize the Bible and was at all the "begats" and I thought that would keep me awake. The "begats" is one of the harder parts. The Book of Job? That's easy. But the "begats?" Oy veh! Suddenly there was a clatter and I was scared at hell because what I saw was this. Moishe in the fireplace (yes, we had one -- an old building --

36

used to be the Marley Hotel I understand -- no gas, no coal furnace) -- but all dressed up in a red and white suit and cursing!

"Where the hell, am I?" Moishe asked.

I knew then it wasn't Moishe and, of course, what I should have done was, well, at least bark at him. But I didn't have time because -- get this -- there wasn't, for that instant (if that makes sense) any such thing as Time. I was frozen in that eternal instant and awake and watching what seemed to me to be a Santa Claus who had, perhaps, put too much rum in his eggnog. In other words I was caught in an eternal timeless instant watching God. Yes. Yes! Yes! Oh, it still affects me so.

Santa seemed confused. He didn't pay any attention to me at all. Just put down a sack he was carrying and looked around with a pissed off look on his face.

Suddenly, the door opened. It was locked and the door opened! And an elf came in.

Santa turned on the elf. "Did you screw up again? Isn't this supposed to be 19 Remington Avenue, Coatesville, Pa, 1958? Well, it looks a lot like a Pawnshop in 1917 to me!"

The elf just looked embarrassed.

"Pull the sled up out front. I'm not going up a chimney if I don't have to."

This is getting a little long.

Well Orson, Santa left. Time was again. I was changed forever. That little encounter with the Eternal changed me forever. I knew who I was and what I wanted to do. Santa left the sack behind and I took out what was in it: a banjo, a unicycle, A Charlie McCarthy doll and the Big/Little Book of English Poetry. Some kid in 1958 wasn't going to have a very nice Christmas. I got a rope from the basement, packed everything in the sack but the unicycle, tied the sack to my back got on the unicycle and hit the road. The rest is show biz history. Somehow I knew where I had to go. I got as far as the old Schubert theatre and cycled right in where some guys were practicing their act. Dec 25, 1917 7AM. Those guys were the Marx brothers. They were a bit surprised.

"I shot an elephant in my pajamas," I said (those were my first English words!)

"How he got in my pajamas I'll never know," Groucho replied. And we both laughed and eyed each other warily. Yes, always that...

My first act: I rode a unicycle and played the banjo while reciting scenes from Shakespeare in Yiddish. This is what I feel formed my sensibility. In other words – I performed America. I was a lousy ventriloquist.

ORSON: Of all your artistic endeavors; films, poetry, music, set and wardrobe design, and on the list goes, which gets most under your fur and why?

RTT: Yes, I did it all. And this will seem strange to you, Orson --after all I am being interviewed because of my work as a poet!-- but what I loved above everything else was Flamenco dancing. As I told you, I didn't know my parents but I love myself for the gypsy soul in me. This is funny. You want to know how I learned flamenco? This is the truth. I learned it with the help of Maria Ouspenskaya when we were making one of those Werewolf movies. I played the wolf -- see him briefly in the moonlight -- that lurks about wanting the soul of the werewolf. Or something! I forget.

Christ, it might even have been "Abbot and Costello meet the Wolfman." But one night Maria took me out to a bar in L.A. I had never been to before. (I didn't think there were any): the "Ola Harpo!" and there I drank Sangria and saw flamenco dancing for the first time.

38

I'm sorry. I'm not very good as an audience and suddenly I was across from a very attractive young gypsy lad with a rose in my teeth. It just came naturally. Oh, how they smiled and applauded as I danced and I was overcome then by the duende. A flash of the tragic divine and I wanted it always and could get it yes I could of nights when the wolfbane bloomed and the moon was large and full and I was dancing with my gypsy friends!

I tried to teach it, off and on, to my Hollywood friends. None of them were any good. But we had a lot of laughs. Bogie almost got it. We would be on his boat with Bacall she laughing as Bogie tried to give himself over to those lunar rhythms and then gave up and he would grab me and bring me close and we would end up doing a tango there on his boat on the sea. A questioning but, perhaps, knowing look on Bacall's face as she watched us and sensed my discomfort. No, I am not implying anything of the usual here. It was Bogie's failure to attain the duende she sensed and my kindness when I covered it up with what was, of course, a COMIC tango. Poor Bogie. Bacall has a new movie I understand.

ORSON: Fascinating, and if we had time, there is much there to be pursued. Yet let us turn, if we may, to your poems of the seventies. Here is one I am fond of:

What a Little Moonlight Can Do

Three days after Bastille day
Behind the shut up café
In a broke down car
(Hard to gas yourself
If the car won't start)
In Cross Plains, Texas
Thinking I saw nothing
More than myself
Reflected in my Les Paul
Black Beauty that night
I step out of my 1971
Ford Maverick the
Door operated courtesy
Light snicking on and
Look up at the sky
At all the tired animals
Stars bluewhitelonely
Thinking of that night
At the Three Deuces so
Long Ago and playing at
The Famous Door
The night Billy died
Errol Garner, Me, Oscar
Pettiford, Errol saying
You better than Django
But nobody will ever say it.
Not knowing Billy was dead
I was happy. Looking up
I say at the skyey animals
The old dog in the moon
Ending like this

Saying to the drunks
In the cowboy bar
This riff is based on Les Negres
By Jean Genet laughing
At myself really and now
Wanting it to end but
The car won't start. Looking
Up I remember I told Billy
Radiance is the dealbreaker
And heard, radio definably off
Her singing "What a Little
Moonlight Can Do" and
That was the last time
I was truly happy and
I was there knowing
I would never try
To find the music again

Tired.

Pancake

Levelland

Mule Shoe

Sonora

Meadow

What vistas of hidden forgetfulness

41

Exhaustively at hand!

This is absolutely splendid, Rinty! The poem crosses so many lines, is inclusive in the way it brings the pathos of the great artist into sharp focus with its carefully chosen images. Bastille Day, of course! One feels the poem begins with the afterparty let down when freedom fails to live up to its promise. And then the emptiness: images of lonely, skywalking animals, brokedown cars behind honkytonk bars. The lacquered cruelty of the Les Paul reflecting it all back at you. And your love dead, unbeknownst to you. And the choppy, riff driven rhythm. Please tell us more!

RTT: Well, it's not exactly an early poem. There were all those poems I wrote with Don Marquis and those horrible "philosophical" poems I wrote after I read Heidegger and then my LangPo stage (met a lot of nice guys byt, really, what was I thinking?) but this lovely poem (and it does everything you say it does and more!) was written around 1985.

The events took place in 1971.

Look, the Bastille day reference is there for several reason. It was the day Lady died and is described just that way in a poem of Frank O'Hara's.

A damn fine poem. Now we go all darkling. Orson, you know I killed O'Hara. Ran him down accidentally while I was drunk and driving a dune buggy on the beach on Fire Island. I recognized him and shouted "O! Frank O'Hara! Look out!" Which, since it follows his style and were the last words he heard, should have been his epitaph.

Why was I drunk and driving a dune buggy at night on Fire Island?

I warn you, Orson we will get into the strange and the very strange as we continue...but let's leave it alone for now.

The events in this poem really happened. This was one of the low points of a long life. I was playing country guitar -- not as Rin Tin Tin but as Merle Shepherd. I wore jeans, cowboy hat, a shirt with little sheep on it, and dark glasses and very uncomfortable Tony Lama Ostrich hide boots and had an act doing Hank Williams covers. I felt I needed to be lost -- I WAS lost. Sometimes I would get paid. Sometimes not. I even robbed a Dry Goods store in Fairy, Texas once when I was hungry and also needed gas. Sometimes I couldn't help it and would play solid gone jazz and sneer at my audience and do an old Lenny Bruce schtick. I slept in my car and there was oblivion and I drank. I'll tell you why later. I get the idea you will know what to ask.

But, yeah, I had the hose hooked up through the window and I was going to poison myself and then the damn car wouldn't start and the radio was off and I anyway heard Billy again there behind the cafe singing that song. And I remembered her for that instant and she was dead but -- and the stars bluewhiteand lonely, the tired animals...we are all so tired when there is death and I realized I shouldn't give myself to death but just go on...

"I was there knowing
I would never try
To find the music again

Tired.

Pancake

Levelland

43

Mule Shoe

Sonora

Meadow

What vistas of hidden forgetfulness
Exhaustively at hand!"

To sleep, perchance to dream, but in that dream...

So it went. But I did try to find that music again. As this poems
shows...as this poem shows.

ORSON: How did you and Billie meet? Where you ever addicted to
heroin?

RTT: No, I never had anything to do with the big H. Even when playing
Jazz guitar. It killed so many of my friends. And my greatest love. I had
a problem with the booze but not until after a certain day in November
1963.

Billy and I met in the late forties at a little Jazz club in Harlem. You
should know, Orson. You went there thinking you were still loved after
your production of the Black Macbeth. I was playing. She came out and
sang from --I don't know -- backstage or Eternity. We fell instantly in
love as she and I became one song as she sang "Strange Fruit."

I guess just the title of that song describes our relationship...

Excuse me for a second, (weeps).

ORSON: When she died on July 17, 1959 you went to Cuba. You wrote this, you told me, looking over the Malecon from your hotel window after going to mass at the Iglesia de San Francisco de Asis over which portal is inscribed non est in toto sanctior orbe locus—no holier place on earth. Castro had just come to power and you wrote:

1953

1953 was a hard year for me.
Sad. I don't know why.
I had work. Me and Bob Mitchum
Were friends at last. After all
Those misunderstandings. "You want to
Break out?" I asked him. "Then forget
All this crap about being a natural actor."
I took his drink away. Got his attention.
"Acting is a craft. Don't scowl at me.
You know I'm right. You'll never
Do Shakespeare unless..." He eyed me warily.
"Yo, Rinty," he said. "You have Billy"
(I had told him) "What do I have?"
He fired up another Chesterfield.
Squinted through the smoke.
"Nothing happens anyway."

Nothing happens?
I knew what he meant.
I was getting there.

He grinned. "How the Hell did you
Do that to McCarthy?"
I gave him back his drink.
"Told him I was a commie, that's how.
"I'm an American Icon, Bob. It was too much for him.
Goodbye Tailgunner Joe."

Bob laughed but he didn't believe me.
He was really quite a charming man
Guys who don't believe in anything often are.
So he could be a gentleman to Rita Hayworth
Down in Mexico, her mind gone. But...
A bastard to everyone else.
Nothing in his eyes.

And I was sad there.
It was New York. September 13, 1953.
Another dive, Another gig.
Bob left with a blonde before I began to play.
 I started to play but just walked out.
It was the night Jimmy and Tommy Dorsey had
Finally gotten together again.
They kept playing while I put down my guitar.

They never forgave me.

 "A" train to Harlem.
Got in Billy's DeSota and drove.

In a few hours
Lost in Pennsylvania.
Stopped. Don't know why.
Got out. Looked up. Falling star.
Not me. Something from forever.

Finally found a town.
Asked a little guy outside a hospital for directions.
"We just had a baby girl," he said.

I drove back to my life.

It seems to me that several important things are happening here. On the poetic level, there is a kind of hyper-realism, a cinematic use of hard focus and quick cuts to close ups, then a pulling away all within the context of a 'dialogue' between you and Mitchum. This severity dissolves toward the end in sadness and loss, and a bone to Creeley, perhaps "driving back to my life".

We are carried along perhaps a bit like a star-struck visitor to Schwabs reading Silver Screen and gaping at celebrity diners. I may be barking up the wrong tree here, but I think there's a deeper movement here. Perhaps it was just the rum?

RTT: There is so much here, Orson. So much strange. Remember those gifts from Santa I picked up in 1917 in that pawnshop in Chicago? The gifts that were to be delivered to a certain address in 1958 in Pennsylvania? Well, those gifts were intended for the young Joe Green! Yes, the poet right here. After my death I communicated through him as a kind of way to make up for the loss of the banjo and unicycle and Charlie McCarthy ventriloquist's dummy and we are and have been cosmically and mythopoetically linked. The last lines in that poem -- well September 13, 1953 is his wife's birthday and the little guy I met outside of the hospital in Pennsylvania was her father and it was that new and blessed and splendid little life that brought me hope again.

The rest -- yes, I brought down McCarthy. If Rin Tin Tin was a communist then nothing meant anything. He never recovered. This is a poem about hope, Orson and damn fine it is that you notice all the slidings and blisses. Thank you.

ORSON: Eventually, you were forced to flea Cuba. What happened with you and Fidel that forced your return to the States

RTT: Do I sense a pun on "flee?" The first time I left Cuba I was sent. We'll get into that. The second time was ...here..here's the poem:

Los Marielitos

You know, Elmore Leonard
got a lot of his Florida schtick from me
when I was sobering up down in Miami.

I guess it was inevitable that I would
get involved with the mob after I fled Cuba
but it didn't start out that way.

May, 1980. They called us Los Marielitos.

I was one of 123,000 new Cuban refugees
that came to the USA in a short five months,
including about 5,000 of us who
were said to be hard-core criminals.

They crossed the ocean on a prayer.

On crowded, unsafe fishing boats.

On rafts held together by tires.

In search of a myth. Carrying only the
clothes on their backs, a passport, and a
crumbled piece of paper with a relative's phone number in the US.

I knew better.

The myth was over for me long ago.

I had Lassie's phone number but of course I would never call it.
She was probably dead and it was a whole new generation and
here I was, the icon of a previous generation, puking half
digested red beans over the side of a raft.

Back in the USA. Back in the USA
done in by the hype back then and by,
yes, my own yen to do serious theatre

Fidel expelled me because I was a drunk, because I was better than he
was and he knew it, because he owed me BIG TIME, because he tried to
kill me but failed and a voodoo curse was placed on his hairy ass that he
could only avoid by getting me out of Cuba. The pretext was that I was
doing street theatre as Trotsky.

ORSON: We have this from that early period by in New York. I
understand you did your own swordplay?

No, I Am Not Prince Hamlet Nor Was Meant To Be

You humans are so predictable.

In fact for years most dogs
were convinced that you were utterly
without self-consciousness -- without Mind.

After all, we present a stimulus to you

49

and we ALWAYS get a predictable response.

The fact is we have such a horror

of the fact

that we can NOT be sincere
that we do whatever we can
to make it stop.

Yeah, a dog will pant
and bark and bring the
damn ball back again and again and again

-- we do it to keep from going mad,
to hope to experience
just for an instant unmediated
unironic consciousness, to --for just one instant
-- be THERE, be in the moment.

It never works.

Never.

That's why we die so young
and it is also why I was,
on a foggy evening OFF OFF Broadway
in a little theatre in the year 1959,

I was, simply put,

the best Hamlet of my generation.

ORSON: Obviously, you were in a philosophical mood here. The poem is quite different than the previous offering. Thoughts are heaved over the transom of regret to drag the depths of your dog nature. Images of Sisyphus and his rock, Skinnerian behavioral psychology, and Buddhist meditation are all brought together in a stunning denouement. Hamlets self-disillusionment is palpable here, yet it doesn't matter that you were "Off Off Broadway" does it? Humans, you seem to be saying, just don't get it. What are we missing?

RTT: This is a poem about consciousness. The first line-- changed at the end by the fact that I was Hamlet -- is Eliot's and is a deliberate deepening of his poem. It gives the facts. Dogs die young because they despair. I saw the eternal so most times I was able to overcome doggy consciousness. See yourself -- humanity -- from a dog's point of view. But I was never one to succumb to the dark.

I did all my own stunts. Always.

ORSON: In 'Road Kill' you seem to have come to some kind of crossroads. Perhaps the intimations of mortality were stronger. We all return to our roots as our time grows short. Here, unlike your other early works, you recognize something of your animal nature:

Road Kill

I ignore them.
The possum squashed on the macadam.
The unprophetic groundhog, in Texas
A holocaust of Armadillos, the skunk

51

"Skunk. God!" you say.
Driving on, a snake absolutely flat on the road.

There is no heaven of animals
A rabbit. A black and white cat.
A small dog stinking in the sun.

You see them and you make up a story.
The dog setting out to warn us all:
Fire, fire in the forest! The turtle there
100 years old!... what thoughts there, Rinty?
And what innocence for all of them.

I'm glad one of us knows the signs
To find our home.

We're all hoping to find our way home in the end. Did your succeed
here in saying what needed to be said?

RTT: This is a poem of divided consciousness. It's again about that
despairing time in Texas. There are two Rintys here. One of us can find
the way home and that way is the way I knew I had to follow. I wanted
to rescue what IS from death. Knew I couldn't so wanted the poem to
say "Seize the Day."

ORSON: This may come as a surprise to you, but we have something
quite special now. Would you read this for us please?

RinTinTology

I never met Django
Never really wanted too, I guess
We would have "eyed each other warily"
Like the time I met Senator Jack Kennedy
Was it 57?
In the Cozy Cole me playing there
Jack with Sammy
Sammy told me he was nervous.
Jack working on his charisma thing
And me.. height of my fame
Billy there Jack wanting her to come to his table
Her not noticing and me looking at her
Playing "Vous et Moi"
Sammy said "Man, come on down see who's here."
So afterwards I sit down next to the Senator
He in black glasses smoking a Kool
Undercover or something
Billie came over. She said she liked the man
Afterwards, knew his Daddy... called him
Mr. Death. "That boy has troubles"
She said. "He was just nervous meeting me"
I told her. She could see that.
Anybody could. "He eyed you warily
Behind those shades" We laughed.
Forgot about it. I had something he wanted.
And he had something...something...
Held back... connection to.. as if he knew
About us, about me and Billy,
Something he said. Joking about Howard Hughes.
Sammy told me Jack laughed afterwards.
"Said he was nervous. Something strange. Didn't

Know why."

In 63 in August Castro "eyed me warily."
A little moonlight, bourbon on his breath,
Backstage, the little moon a paper one
For "Midsummers Night Dream" A wood near
Athens and I had transformed it, a bit of Brecht,
All of Shakespeare, Theseus nervous knowing
That Quince knew, Flute knew, Bottom breaking
the frame, declaring the revolution and me as Puck
Leaping, flying off that stage, like Peter Pan
TO FIDEL he standing up, smiling,
Me kneeling with the flowers but he
Afterwards backstage distant and cold wondering I thought
If the applause was for him or me.

Che was very nice, however.
Speaking one word... one word.
And I was in Dallas next was in Dallas then.

If I could play great jazz guitar
No hand...only paws.
Why couldn't I
Slowly, hold breath, there he is
Pull the trigger
Of a Manlicher-Carcano 6.5mm rifle?

RTT: When I first came to Cuba I founded a wonderful proletarian
theatre and our first play was a version of the Dream. Theseus and the
rest of the ruling class are shot offstage at the end. I played Puck. This
wonderful drawing shows me presenting flowers to Castro.

Castro feared my popularity. Ok. I'll say it. You saw the Manchurian
Candidate? That's what those bastards did to me – they programmed
me so that a certain word would trigger what it did. A few days after
that I was in Dallas. I shot the president. I hope you will post all my
poems in the JD right after that so that the story can be followed with
that insight.

I killed JFK. No wonder I was drunk and playing country guitar all those years. The word was "Rosebud."

ORSON: When I was working on Citizen Kane, I often found myself staying up late and reading Yeats to settle me down. Do you have favorite poets that you turn to? If so, would you share a favorite with us?

RTT: Yeats, Auden, Eliot, the Bard. God bless all poets!

ORSON: Ah, I hear the chimes at midnight! Before we go, however, we must discuss the triad of works that marks your greatness even as you prepared to leave this world. Let's begin with this remarkable view drawing on Homer's great exposition of life's inevitable arc.

Letter from a Dog Before Troy

Dear Penelope,

It's windy here. Nine years in a tent on the beach.
Ulysses says they know what they're doing.

Right.

Nine years and for what?
What's nine years to them?

Most of my life.
I'm tired. Don't even ask me about the gods.
There's a limit to loyalty.

But you already know that.

I know about the puppies.
You should have told me.
She told me, of course.
I don't care.
Just get them out of Ithaca.

By the time you read this
I'll be gone. I have..what..four more years?
Going to someplace where there are no men.
No gods.
Maybe a few rabbits.

Now you go on to treat the great themes of love, death and our position
on the sacred wheel of time. There is bitterness here. God knows your
life has not been an easy one, yet the loneliness of a world without
men? What happened here?

RTT: Now you know. I changed history in a way I would never have
wanted. Am I guilty or not? Somehow I can't feel myself blameless.

Original sin.

ORSON: And yet you then can write:

All the Starry Animals

Looking up
I love them too --
All the starry animals.
Looking down
Or not.
Not saying anything.
Not saying nothing either.

There is a soul clearly in conflict here. Yet in the end there is acceptance. Is it merely what Eliot called " the long looked forward to, long hoped for calm, the autumnal serenity and the wisdom of age" or is there something canine at work here?

RTT: The want for the love that moves the sun and other stars is there.

ORSON: And then there is this:

Old Dog: A Villanelle

I am an old dog and am gently trying,
To meekly go to the difficult dark..
Alone, alone I am slowly dying.

The slow snow drifts down and no wind sighing.
Take out a Zippo and light up a Lark.
No regrets none. No who and no whying.

Sad ghosts outside I hear them all crying.
Mort Sahl's on TV. Makes a funny remark.
No, thanks Time/Life I guess I'm not buying.

Death's at the door. The bastard is lying.
"Hey, Rinty! It's Lassie!" One small sad bark.
Wilder wind now. The snowflakes are flying.

Good Night has come. There is no denying.
Unknown is that country. Stark is the bark.
I am an old dog and am dying, dying.

And you, who haunt me forever sighing,
Crying my name in the difficult dark.

I am an old dog and am dying, dying.
I am alone and am dying, dying.

I am an old dog and am dying, dying.
I am an old dog and am dying, dying

Alone, alone I am slowly dying
I am alone and am dying, dying.

And here we have the only reference in your work to Lassie. Lassie, who was better known, better paid, and more highly thought of than you, if for all the wrong reasons. Beyond that there are echoes of Dylan Thomas' raging against the dying of the light. Clearly the end is at hand. How were you able to do this remarkable work so near to death?

RTT: I never even knew what a villanelle was when I wrote it. The difficult dark – yes! Exactly and here is my epitaph.

I bark at at the dark until the darkness yields.

As you go stark. Babbling of green fields.

Yours,

Rinty

ORSON: And on that noble note, my old faithful friend, our duet is done and for now we must bid adieu. On behalf of our listeners and our sponsor, The Jeunesse Doree, I would like to extend our heartfelt thanks to you, Rinty and wish you Dogspeed!

THE LONELIEST RANGER: And that concludes another exhilarating confrontation of Mr. Orson Welles and the finest minds of today's poetry.

We here at the Jeunesse Doree are pleased to have had you as our guests and look forward to seeing you again.

And please remember to investigate the brilliant, tragi-comic adventures of the lost souls of the JD. Goodnight and have a pleasant tomorrow.

RIN TIN TIN: ARF! ARF!

ABOUT THE AUTHOR

Joe Green was born in Coatesville, Pennsylvania in 1948 and
yet lives. As one can see from the picture of him as a young
cowboy in his book of selected poems" The Loneliest Ranger" (search
"Joe Green" and "The Loneliest Ranger" on Amazon) he had big ears. He
also attended St. Cecilia Catholic School back when attending Catholic
schools was very very strange.

His poem about Sister Eucharista dangling a kid
out a second story window is true although the Blessed Virgin
Mary did not visit his mother so they could drink and watch the
Perry Como Christmas Special together.

Joe got his ears fixed in the sixth grade. Things did not
improve. He went to Bishop Shanahan Catholic High School
in West Chester where, among other accomplishments, he
was caught reading Nietzsche during a prayer retreat. He had
concealed The Portable Nietzsche in a Lives of the Saints cover. This
was in 1963 during the Cuban Missile Crises. Father Schneider
caught Joe reading the guy while taking a break from looking
out the window to see if the Soviet Union had yet sent missiles to
obliterate the school.

Joe graduated in 1966 and went to Marquette University. He
lasted there for one year and was then kicked out because of his
marijuana addiction—which he somehow overcame. Disgraced
and branded, he slunk back home where he was accepted into
Lincoln University in spite of the fact that he had smoked
something someone said was marijuana but he suspected was
electrical bananas as in the Donovan song . Lincoln is the United
States' first degree-granting historically black university. Joe went
there on a minority student scholarship. Langston Hughes is
another poet who attended this institution although, unlike Joe,
he did NOT rack up over $150 in library fines. Joe's immortal friend,
John Rollins. of Burke Road, West Chester can attest to this.

Joe graduated just in time to be drafted. Somewhat reluctant
to go off to Vietnam, Joe enlisted for another year and was

sent to Monterey, California, to learn Russian at the Defense Language Institute. He did learn Russian and was then sent to Fort Huachuca, Arizona, to be a POW interrogator because he refused to sign up for another year. After graduating from there he was chosen to role-play as a Russian POW for Green Berets to interrogate. He was then sent to Fort Hood, Texas, to the 529th MI company (see his Army poems) where he taught English to brides of returning soldiers and was chosen to curate the Army's collection of Bibles in foreign languages, including one in Hawaiian that mysteriously disappeared.

He got out of the Army and went to California to begin his new adventure and ended up briefly selling vacuum cleaners door to door. He re-enlisted and went back to Fort Huachuca where, somehow, he ended up writing Army manuals.

His first publication was not the epic poem about epic stuff he was thinking of writing but was "Nuclear, Biological and Chemical Warfare" in which soldiers were told—no matter what horror unfolded to—"continue the mission."

Joe left the Army after seven years and got a job as a technical writer in Waco (Jerusalem by the Brazos) and then Dallas. Then he got a job at Control Data, Inc. where he helped design and write the first computer-based training ever. He also obtained access to Control Data's "Plato" network of mainframe computers at universities and corporations and at once created a Poetry Newsgroup for persons to post poems, talk about poetry and for him to collaborate with Tim Smith (who lived in Carmel, California and had access to the network) on creating fake comic poets, comic poems and more. Connie, the love of his life, also had access to the system and was amused and saw through it all, so pretty soon Joe moved to Minnesota to be with her. Joe's daughter from a previous marriage also moved up there. Joe flew out to California where he and Tim met, created the "Parapark

Tapes," together and began a collaboration and friendship which resulted in (among much else) the "Limerick Homer."

Joe married Connie in 1990 and their daughter Johanna was born! In Minnesota Joe got a job at Cray Research writing the user's manual for the Cray YMP Supercomputer. Through this job, Joe got access to the USENET: a precursor to the internet and at once spent much of his time contributing to the books and poetry newsgroups. It was here that he met the Great Russian who would eventually publish him in the poetry annual, Fulcrum. Joe also founded the "O'Tooles," This was a blissome group of blissome persons writing blissome this and thats. Joe wrote a story about meeting one of them called "Well Met in Minnesota," which was a big hit ... so much so that there was an article, "Bards of the Internet," about it in Time Magazine. Joe was invited to be a featured speaker at the Third annual Conference on Computers, Freedom and Privacy in San Francisco in 1994 where he extemporized poems about J. Edgar Hoover to an audience of geeks and FBI agents, was told by the head of the Homicide Unit in NYC that he loved his performance, and where he was given a sequence of Star Trek sonnets that were quite good by a lady whose name he wishes he could remember.

Joe then was accepted into the English PhD program at the University of Minnesota. He thought he would be a professor. Ha! He loved it there though and loved his teachers: Chester Anderson, the editor of "Portrait of the Artist as a Young Man," a great Joyce scholar; Tom Clayton, a very great Shakespearean scholar who would oversee the dissertation Joe would never complete; and the guy who was hired in the Sixties, somehow got tenure after publishing a paper on Keats, then, happily, never published anything else. Joe also met Stuart Rieke there, who was a student in a class he taught and is a damn fine poet and musician who composed a song about Joe and the devil and, maybe, Robert Johnson.

Joe returned to work as a technical writer after passing his oral exams and insisting (and carrying it off) that there were hidden depths in Titus Andronicus. Joe had to study The Faerie Queene in depth to pass the exam and sometimes still shows symptoms. Then, in 2002, after renewing contacts with the editors of Fulcrum, he began to be published. His poems appear in every issue of Fulcrum and in one issue of Rattapallax No. 12 (as detailed in the Acknowledgements to this book). He also had three books published by Owl Oak Press: The Diamond at the End of Time (Owl Oak Press, 2006), The Dark Bark: Poetry and Songs of Rin Tin Tin (Owl Oak Press, 2006), The Limerick Homer (Owl Oak Press, 2008).

In August 2012 he began to write his novel The Chains of the Sea (search for it on Amazon! Please!) and finished all 752 pages by November 6, 2012. The novel recounts the quest of "The Visionary Company" to find "The Diamond at the End of Time" and reach God who has not been paying attention. One review says: "Oh my, step aside Samael for Joe Green shall ride on through. With a psychedelic mix of literature culture, music, pop art and motor drama weirdness Joe Green creates a dynamic and engaging fantasy world full of Eliot's cats, dead poets, ray guns and a whole heap besides. There are no illegal substances required with this book as the lines themselves will hypnotize you, spellbind and daze you into an alter-reality, another dimension, well, several all at once with eyes focused on a ragged troupe of disparate travelers through time and space, immortal one feels as they discuss the lengthy and tangled web in which they exist, Godot with a large cast awaiting the final outcome, a mystery to all."

Why did Rin Tin Tin choose Joe?

www.ingramcontent.com/pod-product-compliance
Lightning Source LLC
Chambersburg PA
CBHW060702030426
42337CB00017B/2724